Mastiffs

By Maria Nelson

Gareth Stevens
Publishing

Please visit our website, www.garethstevens.com. For a free color catalog of all our high-quality books, call toll free 1-800-542-2595 or fax 1-877-542-2596.

Library of Congress Cataloging-in-Publication Data

Nelson, Maria.
Mastiffs / Maria Nelson.
    p. cm. — (Great big dogs)
Includes index.
ISBN 978-1-4339-5788-8 (pbk.)
ISBN 978-1-4339-5789-5 (6-pack)
ISBN 978-1-4339-5786-4 (library binding)
1. Mastiff—Juvenile literature. I. Title.
SF429.M36N45 2011
636.73—dc22

                                2010046763

First Edition

Published in 2012 by
Gareth Stevens Publishing
111 East 14th Street, Suite 349
New York, NY 10003

Copyright © 2012 Gareth Stevens Publishing

Designer: Andrea Davison-Bartolotta
Editor: Kristen Rajczak

Photo credits: Cover, pp. 1, 13 iStockphoto/Thinkstock; p. 5 Howard Berman/Getty Images; pp. 6, 17 Shutterstock.com; p. 9 Andersen Ross/Brand X Pictures/Getty Images; pp. 10, 20 iStockphoto.com; p. 14 Image Source/Getty Images; p. 18 Janette Pellegrini/WireImage/ Getty Images.

Printed in the United States of America

CPSIA compliance information: Batch #CS11GS: For further information contact Gareth Stevens, New York, New York at 1-800-542-2595.

Contents

Words in the glossary appear in **bold** type the first time they are used in the text.

Massive Mastiffs

There are many **breeds** of mastiffs. Dogs that are called "mastiffs" in the United States are Old English mastiffs. These mastiffs are giant dogs with smooth coats. They're one of the biggest dog breeds in the world!

There are records of mastiffs dating back to 3000 BC. For many years, mastiffs fought alongside soldiers and helped **protect** people. Today, they're more likely to live with families. Some mastiffs **compete** in dog shows.

Mastiffs are faithful companions.

Dog Tales

The largest dog ever was an Old English mastiff. Zorba was 8 feet 3 inches (2.5 m) from nose to tail.

This mastiff's mask makes it easy to recognize.

▷

Big and Tall

Mastiffs have heavy, square heads and wide chests. They're usually 27 to 36 inches (69 to 91 cm) tall at the shoulder. They weigh 120 to 230 pounds (54 to 104 kg). However, mastiffs can be even bigger than that!

Mastiffs can be **fawn**, **brindle**, or a light orange color. Their coat is short. Mastiffs also have a "mask" of black fur around their eyes, nose, and mouth. They have black ears, too.

The Great Protector

Mastiffs are natural protectors. They don't need training to be good guard dogs. Mastiffs are usually gentle, but they'll act if they sense danger. A mastiff will give a deep bark to scare away someone it thinks may cause harm. Its size alone might be scary to some people!

Mastiffs love their family, but may be less friendly with others. As puppies, mastiffs should meet people and other dogs to learn to accept strangers.

Dog Tales

Mastiffs grow until they're about 2 years old. Too much exercise before then can hurt them.

This mastiff is ready to stand guard.

Today, mastiffs may work with the police or military. ▷

Early Mastiffs

Mastiffs may have been around more than 5,000 years ago. Drawings from that time showing mastiff-like dogs have been found in Egypt and Asia. One of Rome's most famous rulers, Julius Caesar, owned mastiffs. He saw them fighting beside British soldiers in 55 BC and took some to Italy with him. These mastiffs fought bulls, people, and other dogs to please Caesar.

Later, the British used mastiffs for protection from wolves. Nobles had mastiffs guard their castles.

Making of the Breed

Mastiffs almost disappeared in the 1900s because of their huge **appetites**. During World War I and World War II, many people couldn't afford to feed the big dogs. Most were given up or killed. There were few mastiffs in England by the 1940s and 1950s—and they weren't in good health. People brought mastiffs from the United States to save the breed. Some of the dogs were bred with Great Danes and bullmastiffs. This made the breed stronger.

Dog Tales

A mastiff traveled to America on the Mayflower with the Pilgrims.

Bullmastiffs were used to help save the mastiff breed because they come from the same ancient dogs.

13

Mastiffs will be lazy
if you let them! ▷

A Good Companion

Mastiffs are still big and strong like war dogs of the past. But mastiffs today would rather be with their family! They like to live in a house with the people they love the most. Mastiffs learn to obey quickly in order to please their owners.

Mastiffs are usually clean and quiet. However, they need a lot of love and attention from their owners. They can get into trouble if left alone for a long time.

Other Kinds of Mastiffs

There are many kinds of mastiffs. They can be found all over the world. No one knows for sure where the first mastiffs came from. The Old English mastiff is common in England and the United States. This breed may be **related** to other mastiffs, but each breed has its own features.

Tibetan mastiffs have long, soft coats. Neapolitan mastiffs are very wrinkly. Bullmastiffs are shorter and **stockier** than other mastiffs. German mastiffs are best known by another name—Great Danes!

Dog Tales

The Alpine mastiff is another name for a familiar breed—the Saint Bernard.

This is a Neapolitan mastiff.

Dog Tales

To do well in American Kennel Club dog shows, male mastiffs must be at least 30 inches (76 cm) tall and female mastiffs must be at least 27.5 inches (70 cm) tall.

Mastiffs compete in the working dog group at dog shows. ▷

At Work

Mastiffs have been used as guard dogs for thousands of years. Their gentle nature makes them good at other work, too. Mastiffs are excellent **therapy** dogs. Therapy dogs visit people who are sick, lonely, or sad. Therapy dogs and their owners need special training.

Some mastiffs go to dog shows. Mastiffs show off their strength in weight pulling. They also compete in **agility** trials. These mastiffs are judged on how well they move through a course and obey their owner.

Owning a Mastiff

Mastiffs are loving and protective dogs. However, they slobber! Mastiffs have loose lips that drip drool, especially after they eat or drink. They snore, too.

Mastiffs need to play outside and go for walks. They love the extra time owners spend with them outside. Mastiffs' favorite activity is being with their family!

Learning About Mastiffs

height	27 to 36 inches (69 to 91 cm) at the shoulder
weight	120 to 230 pounds (54 to 104 kg)
coloring	fawn, brindle, light orange
life span	10 to 12 years

Glossary

agility: the state of being able to move quickly and easily

appetite: the wish to eat

breed: a group of animals that share features different from other groups of the kind

brindle: having uneven dark bands on lighter-colored fur

compete: try to win

fawn: a light grayish brown

protect: to keep safe

related: two people or animals connected by family

stocky: thick in build

therapy: healing treatment

For More Information

Books

Hart, Joyce. *Big Dogs.* New York, NY: Marshall Cavendish Benchmark, 2008.

Landau, Elaine. *Mastiffs Are the Best!* Minneapolis, MN: Lerner Publishing, 2011.

Websites

American Kennel Club: Mastiff
www.akc.org/breeds/mastiff
Find out more about what mastiffs look like.

Mastiff Club of America
www.mastiff.org
Learn more about owning and showing a mastiff.

Index